2 PETER: LIVING WITH THE END IN MIND

Jonathan Gibson

STUDY GUIDE WITH LEADER'S NOTES

New Growth Press, Greensboro, NC 27401
newgrowthpress.com

Cover Design: Dan Stelzer
Interior Typesetting and eBook: Lisa Parnell
Exercises and Application Questions: Jack Klumpenhower

ISBN: 978-1-64507-327-7 (paperback)
ISBN: 978-1-64507-328-4 (ebook)

Printed in India

29 28 27 26 25   3 4 5 6 7

In Memory of

Andrew ("Drew") Craig

(1929–2022)

Inter multis, proclaimer of Christ's return

CONTENTS

INTRODUCTION

The epistle of 2 Peter is written for a skeptical world, one that belittles God. Such skepticism challenges our faith in two ways. First, it attacks Christian *belief*. It makes us question the most marvelous things about Jesus: Did his miracles really happen? Is he truly the Creator of all things? Is he actually alive? And will he one day return to raise the dead, judge all people, and renew the world? Second, skepticism attacks Christian *behavior*. If Jesus didn't do miracles, what gives him the right to assume he gets to say how we should live? If he isn't our Creator, shouldn't we be looking inside ourselves to define our own identities? And if he isn't returning to judge us and set up a kingdom where his values reign, shouldn't we be making our own progress toward a world with values that feel right to us?

If you live among skeptics, you've heard these questions or may even be asking them for yourself. The Bible anticipates this and addresses it. Peter's brief, second letter targets these exact issues, especially Jesus's outlandishly grand promise to come to earth again. Peter will bring you face-to-face with the Bible's most audacious claims about Jesus—the ones that make people go, "How can you really believe *that*?" You will see both why you should believe such truths and how doing so will thoroughly change your behavior as you wait for Jesus's return.

This means that, as with the other studies in this series, you will pursue godly living by looking constantly at the salvation Jesus gives you. For this particular study, you will focus on a sometimes neglected but vital piece of that salvation. You will see how 2 Peter urges you to be a believer who lives in the present by looking to the future, to live *now* in light of *then*.

HOW TO USE THIS STUDY

This study guide is designed to help you learn from 2 Peter within a small group. Peter's letter is written to believers who are confronting skeptical attitudes, dangerous teaching, and sinful temptations *together*. They need each other for the fight he describes. With this in mind, try to make the group a place where participants feel they can be open about ways the fight is hard rather than having to pretend it's easy. Peter's arguments can be both theologically technical and personally challenging, so also give space for others to take some time, if needed, before they understand or share deeply. Peter has great confidence in Scripture's ability to convince us of the truth. You too should be patient and let it do that for others—and for you.

Each participant should have one of these study guides to join in reading and be able to work through the exercises during that part of the study. The study leader should read through both the lesson and the leader's notes in the back of this book before each lesson begins. No other preparation or homework is required.

There are eight lessons in this study guide. Each will take about an hour to complete, perhaps a bit more if your group is large, and will include these elements:

BIG IDEA. This is a summary of the main point of the lesson.

BIBLE CONVERSATION. You will read a passage from 2 Peter and discuss it. As the heading suggests, the Bible conversation questions are intended to spark a conversation rather than generate correct answers. The leader's notes at the back of this book provide some insights, but don't just turn there for the "right answer." At times you may want to see what the notes say, but always try to answer for yourself first by thinking about the Bible passage.

ARTICLE. This is the main teaching section of the lesson, written by the book's author.

DISCUSSION. The discussion questions following the article will help you apply the teaching to your life.

EXERCISE. The exercise is a section you will complete on your own during group time. You can write in the book if that helps you. You will then share some of what you learned with the group. If the group is large, it may help to split up to share the results of the exercise and to pray, so that everyone has a better opportunity to participate.

WRAP-UP AND PRAYER. Prayer is a critical part of the lesson because your spiritual growth will happen through God's work in you, not by your self-effort. You will be asking him to do that good work.

Peter's rebuke of those who discount God will lead you on a path through some of the Bible's most extraordinary accounts: floods, sulfur and fire from heaven, burned-up planets, a face shining like the sun, and even a talking donkey. Through it all, you will see how the God of wild wonders assures you of his love for you in Jesus and of the mind-stretching immensity of his salvation. Be ready for him to wow you.

Lesson

1

MAKING YOUR SALVATION SURE

BIG IDEA

We should put every effort into godly living, diligently building on all Christ has granted us, while we wait for the coming heavenly kingdom.

BIBLE CONVERSATION *20 MINUTES*

The book of 2 Peter is the Bible's second letter from that apostle. It was likely written to a similar audience as his first letter, to churches in Asia Minor. Peter had been with Jesus and was appointed to lead the church after Jesus ascended to heaven. Peter wrote this letter as he anticipated his own death: "I know that the putting off of my body will be soon" (1:14), which tradition says happened at the hands of the emperor Nero.

Yet despite the persecution from outside the church, Peter's great concern in this letter is dangers inside the church. Peter writes to his fellow believers with an urgent warning. He wants them to resist false teachers who dismiss the Scripture's authority and advocate worldly, sensual pleasures. He urges the believers to keep their focus on the greater pleasures found in Christ. He especially points out how these pleasures are connected to Christ's second coming, the day of the Lord.

Have someone read **2 Peter 1:1–11** aloud or have a few readers take turns. Then discuss the questions below:

The opening four verses describe the life believers have in Christ. What do you find most attractive about the life Peter describes, and why?

Verses 5–7 describe efforts we make as we embrace this godly life. Which of the character traits listed catches your attention, and why? (Focus on the qualities themselves, not the order in which Peter lists them, since he says they all should keep increasing and not just lead to the next in his list.)

Verses 8–11 give reasons why we should work on these Christian qualities. How do Peter's reasons compare to other reasons for living like a Christian that you've heard?

****

Now read the following article, written by this book's author. Take turns reading aloud, switching readers at each paragraph break. When you finish, discuss the questions at the end of the article.

Lesson

CONFIRM YOUR RESERVATION

5 MINUTES

Several years ago, I was flying home from Nairobi, Kenya, and nearly missed my flight because I had not confirmed my reservation. In those days, before there was anything like online check-in, airlines would ask passengers who were flying internationally to phone beforehand and confirm. But I had not phoned. I just presumed I could get on the flight, and then was told when I got to the airport that I most likely could not.

That's what this opening passage in 2 Peter is all about: confirming our place in heaven. "Be all the more diligent to confirm your calling and election. . . . For in this way there will be richly provided for you an entrance into the eternal kingdom of our Lord and Savior Jesus Christ" (vv. 10–11). Picture an Olympic athlete returning home in victory to a welcoming crowd. The Lord Jesus Christ will welcome us home after our victorious Christian life. Peter wants to ensure we catch our flight, so to speak.

Peter's letter includes at least ten explicit references to the coming day of the Lord when Christ will punish the wicked and bring the righteous home. And Peter's point is that you can't get to heaven without hard work. We must "make every effort" (v. 5) and "be all the more diligent" (v. 10). The letter is an exhortation to diligent, godly living while we wait for Jesus's return.

Now, that all sounds a bit like salvation by works, doesn't it? It sounds like salvation might be conditional on practicing qualities like self-control and love that Peter mentions. But notice that the call to be diligent is the *climax* of Peter's opening statement. The *context* begins in verse 1, where Peter says he is addressing those who already "have obtained a faith of equal standing with ours by the righteousness of our God and Savior Jesus Christ." Christ graciously gives the godly life Peter describes. It is a life of equal worth to the life Peter and the other apostles possess.

Such a precious life cannot be earned; it must be received. "His divine power has granted to us all things that pertain to life and godliness" (v. 3). The word *granted* carries the idea of an allocation from a royal bounty. This royal grant we receive is far beyond the ordinary life—breathing, eating, working, playing—that everyone has. Through Christ "who called us to his own glory and excellence," we have been given an extraordinary kind of life. We are Godlike, "partakers of the divine nature" (v. 4).

Peter does not mean we actually become God or a part of God. But our destiny is to be *like* God. We will become immortal, morally perfect, and eternally happy. This is the corruption-free state God originally intended when he made us in his image. Adam failed to raise us up to that life, but Christ has promised it to everyone who comes in faith to him.

Jesus is leading us to a new heaven and new earth where righteousness dwells. This will be a life thick with godly morality, grander than just having Christ's righteousness counted as ours. All our thoughts and desires will actually *be* righteous. We will be free of every evil that corrupts us. We will embody the goodness of our Savior and enjoy the constant happiness of our God. C. S. Lewis wrote that if we were to see now the kind of creatures we will become, we would be tempted to worship them—so like God we will be.[1] John Calvin commented on these verses in 2 Peter by saying we cannot imagine anything more outstanding.[2]

What's more, Jesus has also called us into this life *now*. We have already begun to escape the corruption of our sinful natures. Part of the royal grant is that we get to start practicing a Godlike life today.

This means our effort flows from how Christ has already graciously provided and promised life. How do we respond to that gift of life? Peter says we should supplement or add to it. It's like what we do with our physical life, which came to us from our parents, by grace, without our choice. We supplement that physical life by giving ourselves food, vitamins, sunlight, exercise, and more. We must do this to live. So too, we must add to our Christian life if we love what Christ has given us and expect it to grow.

We never stop receiving, always relying on Christ's work in us. And yet, *we* need to care for our own life too. Peter gives us a list of virtues, like a list of vitamins that will grow our godly life. These counter the self-willed, greedy, sensual indulgence of the false teachers.

There's **faith**, steadfastly relying on Christ and receiving from him. There's **virtue**, which is moral goodness. There's **knowledge**, which here means wisdom and discernment. There's **self-control** and **steadfastness** and **godliness**. There's **brotherly affection**, which is surprising because first-century people used it to speak about blood relations, but Peter says to express it to all believers. And there's **love**, the crowning virtue that encompasses all the others.

This is hard work. With grace comes responsibility. Don't presume on your reservation in heaven; confirm it. You see, the reason I didn't confirm my reservation that time in Nairobi is because I couldn't be bothered to make the effort. I was staying in Tanzania, and I would have had to find a phone and pay for an international call. And so, I only got on my flight by the skin of my teeth.

Here's the difference with the Godlike life: although the life Christ provides for us is one of grace from beginning to end, a true response to that grace is never effortless. No one gets in who does nothing to supplement their Christian life or confirm their calling. So, let us strive to make our calling and election sure.

DISCUSSION *10 MINUTES*

How much is the coming, heavenly life a part of your daily thoughts? Why is that?

What beliefs do you have that Peter would challenge, or what teachings have you encountered that Peter would confront? (For example, have you harbored too small a view of heaven, or the idea that heaven is earned rather than granted, or that grace means the Christian life can be lax, etc.?) Explain.

Lesson

EXERCISE

FOUR MOTIVATIONS

20 MINUTES

Although diligent effort is always part of a true Christian life, that effort flows from the grace of the gospel. At the end of our passage, Peter gives four motivations that can help you be diligent. He anchors these motivations in what Christ has granted and promised.

Each motivation is explained below using a mental picture to help you remember it: a master musician, a blindfold, a bicycle, and a front-row ticket. On your own, read about each motivation. Then pick one that seems especially helpful to you. Take a few minutes to think about why you find it helpful. You might underline or otherwise note parts of the illustration that catch your attention. Be prepared to share your responses at the end of this exercise.

THE MASTER MUSICIAN. "For if these qualities are yours and are increasing, they will keep you from being ineffective or unfruitful" (v. 8).

The first motivation is the promise of a fruitful life. A job well done that makes an impact is hugely satisfying. Imagine Mozart, who composed sublime music we still enjoy today. Or think of someone who plays that music with exceptional beauty. A life that's diligent about imitating Jesus is even more delightful than a Mozart symphony.

When you practice goodness and affection and love, you bring healing and beauty wherever you go. One of Christ's gifts to you is a Spirit-led heart that puts wind behind such a life. In him, you are equipped to master the music of godliness and impact the world for Jesus.

THE BLINDFOLD. "For whoever lacks these qualities is so near-sighted that he is blind, having forgotten that he was cleansed from his former sins" (v. 9).

The blindfold is a negative motivation—a fate to avoid. Peter warns of blind forgetfulness. That's when you stop being diligent and instead get used to your sin so that it starts to master you. You lose sight of how Jesus forgives your sin, releases you from its controlling grip, and has made a sin-free life your destiny. You forget how good godliness is, and you grope in the dark for other pleasures. An awareness that the blindfold is a real danger in the Christian life will help you make an effort to look at Jesus daily and keep following him.

THE BICYCLE. "If you practice these qualities, you will never fall" (v. 10).

If you stop moving on a bicycle, you fall over. But if you keep pedaling, you reach your destination. In the same way, Christians are people who keep moving so as not to fall. The bicycle is a warning against being satisfied with a spiritual standstill—making peace with pet sins or neglecting prayer and God's Word. At the same time, it is also an assurance that Jesus always saves those who do repent of sin and turn to him in faith: *you will never fall*. This promise is yours by grace. It is not based on how far down the road you progress in this life, but on God's pledge that when you keep pedaling through bumps and hills and tiredness you will finish the race upright.

THE FRONT-ROW TICKET. "For in this way there will be richly provided for you an entrance into the eternal kingdom of our Lord and Savior Jesus Christ" (v. 11).

Imagine the most expensive ticket to the grandest game, concert, or exclusive party. Most people would never splurge for such a ticket (if they could even afford the experience at all). But Jesus has richly provided for you to enter his eternal kingdom. He is giving you access to live with him and be like him forever, a life too wonder-filled to imagine fully. When you know the surpassing honor and delight that awaits you, you are able to set aside worldly enticements and be hard-working about godliness.

When the group is ready, discuss the four motivations. Which one do you find especially helpful, encouraging you to be diligent about the godly life? Explain why.

WRAP-UP AND PRAYER *10 MINUTES*

Prayer is for those who know that the entire Christian life, including our effort to obey, is about receiving from God. Together, you will ask your Father for the gifts he loves to grant his children. Be sure to include requests that he will help you to be diligent in the ways described in our passage.

Lesson

2

THE TRUTH ABOUT CHRIST

BIG IDEA

Frequent reminders about the good news of Christ and his return, which God gives us in the Scriptures, help us remain godly while we wait for that day.

BIBLE CONVERSATION *20 MINUTES*

So far in his letter, Peter has written about life in Christ: how we are granted precious promises, how we are called to Christ's own glory and excellence, how we supplement this gift with godly effort, and how we make sure of our entrance into Jesus's eternal kingdom. Now Peter goes on to write about the certainty of that kingdom, which will arrive in its fullness when Christ returns. Peter references some things found in other parts of the Bible:

> **The transfiguration** was an event in the life of Jesus. During most of his time on earth, his full glory as the Son of God was hidden and he appeared no different than any other man. But one time he brought Peter, along with James and John, up a mountain. There his face and clothes became dazzling white like the sun, and those three disciples briefly saw the glory all will

see when Jesus returns. They also heard God's voice declaring Jesus to be his beloved Son with whom he is pleased.*

The prophetic word means all of the Old Testament writings, which persistently point forward to the coming of Jesus. This coming takes place in two parts. Jesus has already come once when he was born, lived, died, rose again, and ascended to heaven. He will also come again to complete his kingdom. The Old Testament writers often had both stages in view when they prophesied about Jesus's coming.

With that background in mind, have someone read **2 Peter 1:12–21** aloud or have a few readers take turns. Then discuss the questions below.

In verses 12–14, notice what's going on in Peter's life and what it makes him want to do. If you were in his situation, how similar might your desires be?

Think of people you know who would consider many events in Jesus's life, like the transfiguration, to be "cleverly devised myths" (v. 16). What parts of Peter's argument might help them believe the whole gospel story?

* The transfiguration is recorded in Matthew 17:1–9; Mark 9:2–9; Luke 9:28–36.

What does Peter say about Scripture that might encourage you to take the Bible even more seriously than you already do? Explain.

****

Now take turns reading this lesson's article aloud, switching readers at each paragraph break.

Lesson

REMEMBER

5 MINUTES

The Christian life includes constant reminders. We're given them throughout the Bible. The Ten Commandments tell us to remember the Sabbath day. The Lord's Supper helps us remember the Lord's death until he comes. And the Lord's Prayer reminds us of our dependence on God as we ask him for our daily bread. These weekly, daily, constant reminders keep us from forgetting the gospel and Christian living.

Peter admits his readers already know about the life and godliness he's just finished mentioning: sharing the divine nature, effort in godliness, and Christ's eternal kingdom. Yet these things are so important that he's determined to remind his readers "always" (v. 12) so they can recall them "at any time" (v. 15). Why the overemphasis on remembering? It's because these gospel realities are *eternal* realities. Peter's impending death is bringing him clarity. He sees what is most important to him, and to us.

In this passage, Peter focuses in on "the coming of our Lord Jesus Christ" (v. 16). He has in mind the second coming, which the false teachers were denying (as we shall see in chapter 3). This is the very thing our secular society today denies—that Christ will return with power and glory. Who do you know on your street, at your work, or at your school who actually lives like the return of Jesus Christ is an imminent reality? Yet Peter assures us that Jesus *is* coming again and that we must remember this. He provides two reasons to be confident of Christ's return.

The first reason is **the apostolic witness to the transfiguration**. You see, the false teachers were saying that the Christian gospel was just concocted stories. They claimed that talk of Jesus being born of a virgin, living under the law, dying on a cross, rising again on the third day, and then coming again at some future point, were all just cleverly devised myths. Perhaps they once believed some of it, and they still believed Jesus existed, but they didn't believe the "supernatural" things about him.

Sure, they agreed that Jesus lived and died. But rose from the dead? Unlikely. Coming again in glory? Hardly. And in fact, both then and now Jesus had not yet returned. So what evidence is there? Well, Peter and the other apostles who were with him could assert with confidence that Jesus is coming in glory because they saw it. God gave them a glimpse of that future when they saw his transfiguration. They also had that glory told to them by the voice of God the Father.

God's announcement at the transfiguration was much more than a fatherly pat on the back. It was a statement of who Jesus is and who he will be. "This is my beloved Son" recalls Psalm 2, where God says his Son will rule all other kings. And "with whom I am well pleased" echoes Isaiah 42, where God delights in his Servant who will bring justice to the nations. Christ's second coming will usher in the fullness of these things, and Peter tells his readers to believe it because he's personally seen it in preview form. We too have this apostolic witness preserved for us in the words of the New Testament.

This brings us to Peter's second reason to be confident Christ is returning: **the prophetic word of the Old Testament**. The rest of the Bible confirms that Jesus will return in power, not only in Psalm 2 and Isaiah 42 but also in passages like Daniel 7:14, where the Son of Man is "given dominion and glory and a kingdom, that all peoples, nations, and languages should serve him" forever.

Again, Peter answers an objection, this time that the words of Scripture are only the writer's own interpretation of things. This too is so relevant for us today. Just try to witness to your friends about Jesus by quoting Scripture. How will they respond? They will likely say the Bible is a human document, not fully reliable, at best one part or one point of view of what God might be saying to us. They will say it's humanly inspired, perhaps even cleverly conspired.

But Peter says the Scripture writers were "carried along," or "borne," by the Holy Spirit. It's the same word he uses for the very voice of God from heaven in verses 17 and 18. The imagery is of a ship carried by the wind. The prophets opened up their sails, so to speak, and the Holy Spirit filled them. What they wrote, God wrote.

I once visited Professor David Gooding, a renowned Bible teacher in the UK, and he made a comment that has remained with me. He said we should so study Scripture that we are convinced of what the text is saying, so that if "God were to open up heaven and speak audibly to you, he wouldn't have anything else to say." In other words, what Scripture says is what God says. This is why we pay such attention to the whole Bible, Old and New Testaments. Scripture is divine light, God speaking to us in the here and now, telling us everything he has to say.

With that certainty in place, we need to ask ourselves what the connection is between Christ's future return and how we live as Christians today. The future always influences the present. Just think of Christmas Day every year. Ahead of time we save money, buy gifts, invite guests, and prepare a meal. As the day approaches, it affects our everyday lives.

How should Christ's pending return affect our daily lives? Peter has already told us in the previous section: we ought to live diligent, godly lives while we await the eternal kingdom of our Savior Jesus Christ. It is his glorious kingdom that changes everything. Our job is to remember.

DISCUSSION *10 MINUTES*

When in your life have you received reminders about Jesus, and how have they affected you?

Sometimes our regular use of the Bible (for personal or group reading and study, or hearing it preached) can come to feel guilt-driven or stale. But Peter treats it as a refreshing light in a dark world. What is your own experience with how it feels to use the Bible regularly? How has that experience changed, or how would you like it to change?

FUTURE EVENTS, PRESENT-DAY EFFECTS

20 MINUTES

Peter says God's Word is your light in a dark world that denies Jesus's return, your lamp of remembering until Jesus ends the darkness. So for this exercise, you will work on your own to use passages from the Bible that remind you of what will happen when Christ returns.

Begin by reading through each Bible passage below. Note several things God is telling you that might change your everyday behavior if you always keep them in mind. Then pick a specific part of your everyday life, and consider how you might act differently when you think about Christ's return during that part of your day. Be ready to share and explain your results at the end of the exercise.

STEP 1: What you will remember. Read the passages and underline or otherwise note parts that seem especially helpful or life-changing.

Jesus's return will bring the joyous completion of the mission to preach Christ to all nations. "They will deliver you up to tribulation and put you to death, and you will be hated by all nations for my name's sake. . . . **But the one who endures to the end will be saved. And this gospel of the kingdom will be proclaimed throughout**

the whole world as a testimony to all nations, and then the end will come" (Matthew 24:9, 13–14).

Jesus's return means everyone will see his glory and his triumph over evil. "The powers of the heavens will be shaken. And then they will see the Son of Man coming in a cloud with power and great glory. Now when these things begin to take place, straighten up and raise your heads, because your redemption is drawing near" (Luke 21:26–28).

When Jesus returns, your body will be resurrected and will take on a new, Godlike life. "What is sown is perishable; what is raised is imperishable. It is sown in dishonor; it is raised in glory. It is sown in weakness; it is raised in power. It is sown a natural body; it is raised a spiritual body" (1 Corinthians 15:42–44).

When Jesus returns, wrongs done against him and you will be repaid. "God considers it just to repay with affliction those who afflict you, and to grant relief to you who are afflicted as well as to us, when the Lord Jesus is revealed from heaven with his mighty angels in flaming fire, inflicting vengeance on those who do not know God and on those who do not obey the gospel of our Lord Jesus" (2 Thessalonians 1:6–8).

Jesus's return will bring eternal life for believers and eternal judgment on the devil and his followers. "And I saw the dead, great and small, standing before the throne, and books were opened. Then another book was opened, which is the book of life. And the dead were judged by what was written in the books, according to what they had done" (Revelation 20:12).

Jesus's return will bring you into never-ending life with God and with those who are righteous. "Behold, the dwelling place of God is with man. He will dwell with them, and they will be his people, and God himself will be with them as their God. He will wipe away every tear from their eyes, and death shall be no more, neither shall there be mourning, nor crying, nor pain anymore, for the former things have passed away" (Revelation 21:3–4).

Jesus's return will usher in a new creation free of every corruption and undisturbed by sin. "No longer will there be anything accursed, but the throne of God and of the Lamb will be in it, and his servants will worship him. They will see his face, and his name will be on their foreheads. And night will be no more. They will need no light of lamp or sun, for the Lord God will be their light, and they will reign forever and ever" (Revelation 22:3–5).

STEP 2: <u>When</u> or <u>where</u> you will remember. Pick one specific part of your everyday life in which remembering these truths might change how you act.

☐ A part of my life at work/school: ______________________________

____.

☐ A part of my life at home: ______________________________

____.

☐ A part of my life at church: ______________________________

____.

☐ A recurring situation with my family: ______________________

____.

☐ A regular part of my life with friends: ______________________

____.

☐ Other: ____

____.

Briefly note how your behavior might change when you remember Christ's return at these times in your life. ____________________

____

____.

When the group is ready, explain and discuss your answers. What are some specific ways remembering the future event of Christ's return will affect your present-day life as a believer?

WRAP-UP AND PRAYER *10 MINUTES*

Praying for Christ to return and finish establishing his eternal kingdom is part of the Christian life: "Your kingdom come" (Matthew 6:10) and "Come, Lord Jesus!" (Revelation 22:20). For your prayer time together, you might include anticipatory prayers for that day to arrive. Also pray that God would keep you mindful of the godly living and kingdom work he has given you to do in the meantime.

Lesson

3

DANGEROUS TEACHING

BIG IDEA

False teachers are dangerous, always leading the church into sin and away from the Savior, and they must be eliminated.

BIBLE CONVERSATION *20 MINUTES*

Peter has just finished writing about Old Testament prophets who spoke from God, and now he moves from that into the central concern of his letter. False prophets also exist, he says, and they are terribly destructive. Remember that the teachers who concern Peter doubted (1) the supernatural truths about Jesus and (2) the Bible's authority as straight-from-God instruction. This meant they looked to sensibilities found within their culture, instead of to what God says, when deciding right from wrong—and they lived for feel-good pleasures. Sadly, similar teaching is still found today, sometimes even from those who might call themselves Christian pastors.

One of Peter's points will be that God surely brings a greater destruction back onto those false teachers, but that will be the theme of our next lesson. For this lesson, focus your attention not on how false teachers get destroyed but on how they might destroy us. Begin by having someone read **2 Peter 2:1–3** aloud. Then discuss the questions below:

Look for clues to the personal character of the false teachers. What about their character especially bothers you, and why?

When false teachers are in the church, how does Peter want us to think of them? How does this compare to attitudes you've seen in churches today?

Peter says, "the way of truth will be blasphemed," meaning the Christian life will fall into disrepute because of the sinful behavior of supposed Christians. What kinds of damage have you seen result from this?

****

Now read the article from this book's author. Take turns reading aloud by paragraph, and then discuss the questions that follow.

Lesson

THE TRAITS OF FALSE TEACHERS

5 MINUTES

A few years back, an evangelical organization where I lived put on a debate. It pitted a Christian professor at a well-known university, who was also an ordained minister, against an atheist professor. At one point, the Christian minister was asked an easy question meant to let him defend the evidence for Christ's resurrection. I can still remember what he said instead: "Of course, when we Christians talk about the resurrection, we're not saying that Jesus *literally* walked out of the grave in a bodily fashion. We're just speaking about a spiritual resurrection of some kind."

A few weeks later, the committee of Christians who had planned the debate invited me to meet with them. The meeting began with discussion about how the debate had gone, and the response was generally positive. When I raised a concern about the Christian minister denying the bodily resurrection of Christ, one person on the committee said, "Oh yes, I mean, apart from the heterodoxy, I think it was a great success. We all knew that minister was a bit heterodox, but the debate got the most downloads on the internet we've ever had!"

What struck me that day was not an *inability* to discern false doctrine. The gentleman on the committee admitted this minister was heterodox—out of line with right doctrine. No, what struck me was the *indifference* and *apathy* toward false doctrine. In the Bible, false teaching is never a matter of indifference or apathy. It is serious business. False prophets and false teachers get damned for it.*

That's because false teaching is a deadly virus that attacks the organism of Christ's body, the church. Peter repeatedly says these heresies lead to "destruction." In the New Testament, the word he uses often means damnation to hell. The response of Christ's body to such viruses should be to identify them and then eliminate them. The church must have a doctrinal immune system.

False teachers will always be with us. Peter points out how they have hidden among God's people since Old Testament days. In fact, it all began in the garden of Eden with the first false teacher, the serpent—Satan himself—who twisted God's words, leading to death. With so much at stake, Peter uses the opening verses of chapter 2 to help us identify false teachers and see why they are so dangerous. He gives us four characteristic traits.

1. Underhanded agendas. False teachers secretly bring in destructive teaching from the outside. In Peter's day, these false teachers were probably influenced by Epicurean philosophy in Greco-Roman culture, and they wanted to introduce it into the church. The Epicureans claimed there was no God providentially controlling the world or speaking truth into it, meaning we should live for pleasure and sensual indulgence.[3] This teaching did not arise from Scripture but was brought in from outside. That's the great danger in all attempts to integrate secular thinking with Christian doctrine. Just read church history: taking direction from outside philosophies always leads away from orthodox doctrine and a Godlike life. First you reject the Bible's miracles, and soon you rethink its morality.

* For example, see Deuteronomy 13:5; Jeremiah 23:14–15; Matthew 7:13–15; Galatians 1:8.

2. Fake belief. False teachers are, or once were, professing believers. Peter even speaks of them in a way that sounds like Christ had saved them, since outwardly they looked connected to the Savior. But inwardly, something very different was going on, and their outward connection to Christ made their indulgent behavior and false teaching all the more damnable. Of all people, they should have known better. Their fakeness made them that much more accountable.

3. Disgrace on the church. False teachers are popular and have followers. This means they cause the way of truth to be blasphemed. In Peter's case, the false teachers' wrong beliefs about Christ—that he will not return in judgment—led them into an unchristian lifestyle. They concluded it was okay to be a Christian and get drunk, sleep around, and so on—much like many who profess Christ today. The effect of such living is that other Christians are led astray into similar lifestyles. Then onlookers start to associate Christ with those lifestyles. The way of truth suffers disgrace.

4. Greedy exploitation. The attitude of false teachers is not sacrifice but greed. They don't seek to serve others, only themselves. Like some wealth-and-prosperity preachers today, Peter says the false teachers exploit people with fabricated, plastic words. Those who accuse the apostles of manufacturing myths about Jesus are actually the ones inventing false words. Those whom Christ supposedly bought are now trying to make money off those he truly bought, exploiting Christ's own people.

All of this is what false teachers do. That day during the debate, when the so-called Christian minister denied the bodily resurrection of Christ, a deadly doctrinal virus was disseminated in the lecture hall and later through the internet. All that minister did was lead people one step closer to hell.

His comments were all the more damnable because he knew better. He was ordained in a denomination whose doctrinal statement affirms the bodily resurrection of Christ, as the Bible does repeatedly.* On top of that, one of the biggest disgraces was that he received an honorarium when he had failed to do what he was invited to do—defend the Christian faith. He got paid for a heresy, and those are never harmless or neutral—they're destructive. May God build the immune system of Christ's body so that we can identify such people who would draw us away from trusting Christ and from the Godlike life.

DISCUSSION *10 MINUTES*

When have you had apathy or indifference to false teaching? Why do you think you responded that way?

What other emotional responses do you have to false teaching? Do any of its four characteristics make you feel angry, discouraged, self-righteous, etc.? Explain.

* See Luke 24:36–43; John 20:24–29; Acts 2:24–32; 10:40–41; 1 Corinthians 15:3–20, 35–49.

Lesson

FALSE TEACHING IN YOUR LIFE

20 MINUTES

For the false teachers in 2 Peter, wrong ideas about Jesus led to a warped relationship with sin. This is no surprise. Since Jesus is your utterly thorough Savior from sin, any departure from what the Bible says about him can only lead to a too-small view of his victory over sin or to accommodation in the fight against sin.

On your own, read the examples of *gospel truth* about how Jesus saves you from sin. Also read the examples of *false teaching* that might deny or downplay each truth, leading you to underappreciate Jesus or disregard sin's danger. As you read, look for two things:

1. Note which false teachings you may have heard, either directly or implied, and may have believed either now or in the past.
2. Note any false teachings you may realize are wrong but still are a direction you tend to lean when you forget the gospel.

Be prepared to share your responses at the end of the exercise.

GOSPEL TRUTH: Jesus saves you from sin's death grip. By Christ's transforming power, as a believer you are no longer under sin's control but are now spiritually alive. You are able to obey God, trust him as your Father, and grow as you respond to his Word.

FALSE TEACHING might reject the idea that you were ever under sin's control or unable to be a good person. It prompts you to praise yourself rather than Jesus for any devotion you show to God or good behavior that gets noticed.

FALSE TEACHING might be so fixated on admitting sin and being authentic about struggles that you avoid the real power God gives you to repent of sin daily (which includes true sorrow and turning). You talk about forgiveness but neglect your duty as God's dearly loved child to make every effort to grow in godliness.

GOSPEL TRUTH: Jesus saves you from sin's condemnation. On the cross, Christ took all the shame and punishment you deserve, in your place. In return, he gives you his righteous record. Solely through faith in him, you are forgiven, adopted as God's child, and made an heir of eternal life.

FALSE TEACHING might dismiss the fact that God punishes sin or that your sin is bad enough to deserve his wrath. It reduces the cross to a symbol, makes your salvation feel routine, and ignores the urgency of evangelism.

FALSE TEACHING might overemphasize *what you must do*, or some external step or rite, so that in effect it bases your salvation on what you earn rather than what Christ gives you. You end up measuring God's love for you by your performance rather than by the worth of Jesus's sacrifice.

GOSPEL TRUTH: Jesus saves you from a sinful lifestyle. By his Spirit, Christ performs a spiritual and moral renewal in you. He works throughout your life to make you more like him, so that you put sinfulness to death and embrace a godly life.

FALSE TEACHING might downplay the glory of being someone who listens to Jesus when deciding right from wrong, and who is on his side against sin in every way and in every part of life. You belittle efforts to be holy or you treat daily repentance as optional—or even unhealthy.

FALSE TEACHING might treat holy living as a matter of self-effort rather than cooperation with Christ's work in you. Your Christian life feels self-powered rather than dependent on prayer, God's Word, and his gifts received through his church—and you limit your obedience to what feels doable.

GOSPEL TRUTH: Jesus saves you from sin's curse in the world. Jesus will return to completely defeat evil and death, undo every spoiling effect of sin, and finish establishing his perfectly righteous kingdom.

FALSE TEACHING might overlook any real hope in Jesus's supernatural crushing of evil. You replace hope in Jesus with an empty hope focused on this world's leaders or limited to present-world progress.

FALSE TEACHING might disregard the real value of doing good in the world today in Jesus's name. You fail to realize the greatness of being on mission and working now for a kingdom that will one day have eternal grandeur.

One false teaching I have heard and/or believed is: ______________

____

____.

One false teaching I lean toward even though I know better is:

____

____.

When the group is ready, share your responses. Try to include some context or examples, explaining how you think each false teaching got a foothold in you.

How might the truth about Jesus and the message of 2 Peter help you eradicate the false teaching from your life?

WRAP-UP AND PRAYER *10 MINUTES*

You might pray for the gospel to be proclaimed and heard with truth and fullness, both in your own life and elsewhere in the world.

Lesson

4

DESTRUCTION AND SHELTER

BIG IDEA

God surely will judge evildoers and rescue the righteous, as he has shown in the past.

BIBLE CONVERSATION *20 MINUTES*

In chapter 2 of his letter, Peter is combatting false teachers. Our last lesson focused on how false teachers destroy the church, and this one will look at how God plans to destroy them. As you read further into the chapter this time, you will encounter references to mass destruction from some of the earliest parts of the Bible.

God's judgment of the angels is most likely a reference to angels who rebelled against God's authority long ago and were cast out of heaven.

Noah lived during a time when wickedness became so great that God decided to destroy humanity with a worldwide flood. Only Noah, who was righteous, was saved in an ark along with seven family members (Genesis 6–9).

Sodom and Gomorrah were wicked cities in the time of Abraham, whose nephew **Lot** made the foolish choice to live in Sodom. God came to destroy the cities, and two angels were guests at Lot's house when all the men of Sodom came to force sex on them, thinking the angels were ordinary men. Lot pleaded with the crowd not to do that wickedness, but the mob said he had no business judging them and threatened him in return. The angels intervened, and Lot and his daughters were able to flee the citywide destruction as God rained sulfur and fire from heaven the next morning (Genesis 19).

With that background, have someone read **2 Peter 2:1–10** aloud or have a few readers take turns. Then discuss the questions below:

What are Peter's main points that lead him to write about sweeping examples of God's judgment? How does his decision to do that make you feel?

How does Peter's use of the Bible accounts—the flood and Sodom and Gomorrah—compare to other ways you've heard those stories taught?

Imagine quoting verses 9 and 10 in a public place where you live. What might be the reaction, and why?

****

Now read aloud the following article, switching readers at each paragraph break. Then discuss the questions at the end of the article.

Lesson

ARTICLE

NO IDLE WARNING

5 MINUTES

One time as children living in Tanzania, my brother and I climbed onto the roof of a neighbor's house despite our father having explicitly told us not to. He warned there would be severe consequences if we did. Sure enough, one day we decided to climb the neighbor's roof while our dad was at work, but our muddy footprints gave us away and we got caught. Our mother sent us to our bedrooms with the words, "Wait there till your father comes home." It was probably the longest afternoon of our lives. Why? Because we knew our father's words were no idle warning. His discipline surely was coming.

That's what this section of 2 Peter is all about: God's coming judgment, which is no idle warning. The false teachers who followed their defiled passions didn't believe in divine judgment. But just as "he who keeps Israel will neither slumber nor sleep" (Psalm 121:4), Peter says God will not slumber nor sleep over false teachers.

To show the certainty of this, Peter presents us with three examples from history. These biblical judgments are more than just events that once happened in the past. They also serve as prophetic enactments of the future, "an example of what is going to happen to the ungodly" (v. 6). They are signposts of the day Jesus surely will come as Judge.

First, *God did not spare sinful angels.* The angels here are most likely those who rebelled with Satan (then Lucifer) in heaven, rather than the "sons of God" who went in to the daughters of men in Genesis 6. Peter's point is that God did not allow these angels to get away with whatever they did.

Next, *God did not spare the ancient world before the flood.* The Bible says, "The Lord saw that the wickedness of man was great in the earth, and that every intention of the thoughts of his heart was only evil continually" (Genesis 6:5). We also read that the earth was violent and "corrupt in God's sight" (Genesis 6:11). As wickedness grew, God was not idle nor asleep. He saw it and judged it.

Finally, *God did not spare Sodom and Gomorrah.* Genesis 13:13 says "the men of Sodom were wicked, great sinners against the Lord" well before the incident at Lot's house. That included perverting the practice of God's good gift of sexual relations between a married man and woman. Notice how sexual lust and despising authority go hand in hand in verse 10 of Peter's letter. Every sex-distorting movement of our culture can be summed up in the serpent's words in the garden: "Did God really say?" *Who says I can't sleep with that person?* God's response: "If you disobey what I have commanded, judgment is coming."

Now a question naturally arises: If the flood destroyed the whole world, and if fire destroyed the whole cities of Sodom and Gomorrah, what hope is there for us? We live in a world that is similarly wicked. How shall we escape the coming, even more widespread, judgment? This is why Peter mentions the two righteous men, Noah and Lot.

Despite living in a time of increasing wickedness, Noah had opportunities to preach righteousness. And despite living in a time of destruction, Noah was saved—and he was not alone. Some translations refer to "seven others," but the original wording calls him "Noah the eighth." Not only was he the eighth person saved from the flood, the number eight also signifies the first day of a new week. It's a symbol for a new beginning out of destruction—a new world, like Jesus will establish when he returns.

Peter's mention of Lot is perhaps even more encouraging. If you read Genesis, "righteous" is not the word you might use to describe Lot. He chose to live in Sodom because it looked good, despite knowing it was full of wickedness. He also tried offering his daughters to the lust-filled men pounding down his door, suggesting they do whatever they pleased to the daughters instead of to his visitors. He was a terrible moral failure before God.

This means the statement about Lot's righteousness must mean his *positional* righteousness. As with Abraham, God credited Lot with righteousness because of his faith, and preserved his disdain for evil. Lot made many sinful choices in life, but by grace he still had a moral compass and never lost his righteous state before God—and he was saved amid the destruction from heaven.

You may ask, "How do I escape the coming judgment? How can I be on team Noah and team Lot?" Well, before a storm there are always signs—distant thunder and threatening wind. They are our chance to get indoors, to get to safety. And in history and in our lives, God does the same. He gives precursors of judgment ahead of the main event. These are signs that we should get into the ark like Noah or flee the city like Lot.

Our place of safety is a person, Jesus Christ. When he died, he absorbed the wrath of God on our behalf. When Jesus died, a clip of God's future judgment was released early. It fell on Jesus instead of on all who have faith in him. We each need to ask ourselves where we will be found when the final storm of judgment arrives. Will we be inside or outside? Will we be hiding in Christ or caught in the flood and fire? Because God makes no idle warnings, nor any idle promises. His coming judgment is certain, and so is his coming salvation for those who are in Christ.

DISCUSSION *10 MINUTES*

When in your life have you needed to be reassured that God is not asleep?

What precursors of judgment has God graciously put into your life, getting your attention so that you seek shelter in Jesus?

Lesson

NOAH, LOT, AND PETER

20 MINUTES

As you've seen, the Bible gives accounts of real people who have struggled in the world. This lesson's Scripture has put you inside the lives of Noah and Lot, and of Peter who wrote about them. Their concerns and hurts as they lived amid ungodliness, and their feelings in the face of God's judgment, can help you understand your own.

Below, work by yourself to record how much your feelings match what Noah, Lot, and Peter seem to have felt. Read each statement and rate how true it is of you, assigning it a 1 if it is not at all true of you, up to a 5 if it is very true of you. Then move on to read about God's answer to these hurts and concerns. NOTE: Sharing your results with the group will require some openness about your personal worries. You won't necessarily have to talk about every item. Be sure to be honest with yourself as you complete this exercise, knowing that you can pick which answers to reveal to the whole group.

☐ 5 ☐ 4 ☐ 3 ☐ 2 ☐ 1 **Noah's isolation.** Like Noah, I feel like a frustrated herald of righteousness. The whole world seems ever more committed to evil and refusing to listen, and I feel helpless and alone.

☐ 5 ☐ 4 ☐ 3 ☐ 2 ☐ 1 **Noah's concern for family.** Like Noah, I am anxious about my own "seven others." I have sadness or fear about my family and friends being hurt in a godless world or lured away from the Savior.

☐ 5 ☐ 4 ☐ 3 ☐ 2 ☐ 1 **Lot's righteous distress.** Like Lot, my heart is torn up over all the sensual conduct and lawlessness I see and hear around me. My pleadings only end with people threatening, "Don't judge me!" It scares me and it eats at my soul. The world I now live in feels painful to me.

☐ 5 ☐ 4 ☐ 3 ☐ 2 ☐ 1 **Lot's sinful culpability.** Like Lot, I might be haunted by my own guilt. I know I've moved too close to the evil and sensuality around me, or have indulged in it. I realize I share blame for my family's troubles or other's hurts. I wonder if God will really count me righteous when he sends his angels to execute judgment.

☐ 5 ☐ 4 ☐ 3 ☐ 2 ☐ 1 **Peter's concern for the church.** Like Peter, I am disturbed about the direction of the church. I am alarmed by how it accepts the world's philosophies and sensual behaviors, or how it ignores the gospel and a Godlike life.

☐ 5 ☐ 4 ☐ 3 ☐ 2 ☐ 1 **Peter's anger over evil.** Like Peter, I am angry at people who have hurt those I love or have led them astray, or at people who have hurt me—perhaps even within the church. I ask, "Will God ever make this right? Can he really give me justice?"

Next, consider what our passage says about how Jesus will both punish the wicked and rescue the godly. Read through the items below. As you wait for the group to finish, start thinking about how these truths might address your worries.

- God's condemnation is not idle and he is not sleeping through this (v. 3).

- No sin escapes punishment; Christ either will fully punish the evildoer or has fully absorbed the punishment for the sinner who turns to him (vv. 4–6).
- God preserves a witness to righteousness in the world even when immorality is at its worst (v. 5).
- Distress over sin is a righteous attribute, and the Lord rescues the righteous (vv. 7–8).
- All is not hopeless; the Lord knows how to free his people from all the trials and dangers of sin (v. 9).
- The Lord is restraining evildoers, already keeping them under partial punishment until he returns to judge them fully (v. 9).
- Those who do harm by indulging their lusts and despising God's authority will one day tremble before him (v. 10).

Now share and explain some of your results. What concerns or hurts do you share with Noah, Lot, or Peter? Do you notice any patterns?

How do the truths about Jesus address your concerns and hurts?

WRAP-UP AND PRAYER *10 MINUTES*

One key fact about our complaints, worries, and hurts is that God invites us to tell him about them. Spend some time in prayer, sharing the results of the exercise with your Father. Ask him to heal your hurts, do justice, rescue you from sin, and supply all you need.

Lesson

5

ARROGANT MADNESS

BIG IDEA

Anyone and anything that draws us away from Christ is a stain and an empty promise, deserving condemnation, which the Bible sometimes expresses in stark ways.

BIBLE CONVERSATION *20 MINUTES*

Remember that the false teachers Peter is denouncing are driven by an agenda that's based in the surrounding culture rather than the gospel found in the Bible. They might still affirm selected truths about Jesus, but their real passion is the pleasure-affirming viewpoint they've latched onto. Now in this lesson's passage we will see how even that isn't really what drives them.

To understand the passage, it will help to be familiar with the Bible's account of the pagan prophet Balaam. Balak, the king of Moab, tried to hire Balaam to put a curse on God's people because Balaam had a reputation as a powerful shaman. Although the Lord told Balaam not to do it, the king's promise of a large payment eventually got Balaam on his donkey and traveling to the job. When the angel of the Lord came with a sword and stood in the road to oppose Balaam, only the donkey could see the angel. Three times the donkey took action to avoid the angel, embarrassing Balaam but saving his life without him realizing it.

> And Balaam's anger was kindled, and he struck the donkey with his staff. Then the Lord opened the mouth of the donkey, and she said to Balaam, "What have I done to you, that you have struck me these three times?" And Balaam said to the donkey, "Because you have made a fool of me. I wish I had a sword in my hand, for then I would kill you." And the donkey said to Balaam, "Am I not your donkey, on which you have ridden all your life long to this day? Is it my habit to treat you this way?" And he said, "No." (Numbers 22:27–30)

Now have someone read aloud what Peter says about false prophets in **2 Peter 2:10–22**, or have a few readers take turns. (The passage will start with a reference to "the glorious ones," meaning angels, one of the supernatural things the false teachers scoffed at.) When you finish reading, discuss the following questions:

Peter sounds angry. Based on his description of the false teachers, how would you defend Peter's right to be angry about them?

What about Balaam do you find worthy of dislike or ridicule? How is that a fitting example of what the false teachers are like too?

Verses 17–19 describe false teachers as "waterless springs." How do these verses fit your own experience with worldly attractions or viewpoints that promise life but don't deliver?

****

Next, read the article aloud, taking turns by paragraph, and then discuss the questions that follow it.

Lesson

ARTICLE

IN DEFENSE OF DENUNCIATIONS

5 MINUTES

The book of 2 Peter has sometimes been called the ugly stepchild of the New Testament. That's partly because it's filled with judgments and denunciations of the false teachers. In this passage, Peter even says they are so stupid a donkey would know better. That does sound a bit abrasive. But I want you to start asking yourself if perhaps it's actually healthy. Let's look at why false teachers deserve to be denounced.

First, their starting point is that they are arrogant and irreverent. They are rationalists, putting their own reasoning and the world's "evidence" ahead of what God says in the Bible. In Peter's case, the false teachers denied anything supernatural or spiritual, dismissing talk of angels as irrational and ridiculous.

Peter exposes their underlying attitude. He notes that the heavenly angels themselves would not speak in the same dismissive way about the false teachers. Why not? The angels actually *know their place* "before the Lord" (v. 11). In contrast, any thinking that tests the Bible by our own wisdom *assumes the place of God*. It is inherently arrogant and blasphemous.

This means that anytime we go around claiming to be made in God's image so that we're rational and wise, but our thinking hasn't come from God, we are actually no better than irrational animals. We're led by instinct, not intellect. We talk nonsense, not sense. We're bound for death, not the Godlike life. This is because non-Christian thinking of whatever stripe—religious, philosophical, scientific, even much of what goes by the name *Christian*—has cut itself off from the God who is light.

We mustn't miss how direct and in-your-face this is. Peter goes on the attack, cutting to the heart of the matter. No matter how rational we might think we're being, anyone not humbly led by God's wisdom is actually being driven by sinful desires. Such people have "eyes full of adultery" and "hearts trained in greed."

Peter chooses Balaam to underscore his point. Not only was Balaam eager to curse the Israelites for money, he later was influential in enticing them to sleep with foreign women.* He illustrates both drives—sex and money. The result was that Balaam, who postured as such a spiritually wise man, had a donkey who actually knew better than he did. Balaam was so driven by his instinctual greed that he was no longer thinking straight.

There's a lesson here for us when we engage in arguments about Christianity and how a Christian should live. There's usually a lifestyle desire underneath. What really drives people's viewpoints is not reason but a desire to do what gives them pleasure. If you start pursuing the love of money, or start playing around with sexual pleasures outside of marriage, you'll also start to read your Bible differently—or you may stop reading it altogether. You'll build for yourself a "rational" framework that allows you to live as you please.

This means it's easy to start believing false teachers or to follow our culture when they tell us these desires are helpful. But Peter insists

* See Numbers 25:1–3; 31:16.

they are not helpful, but harmful. They are "waterless springs" (v. 17). They promise refreshment and life, but they don't actually quench our thirst. They are "mists driven by a storm," which seem to bring cooling relief for a moment but are quickly blown away—and useless. They promise freedom but deliver slavery. They affirm pleasure but deliver prison.

And when it comes to teachers who hold out these empty promises, we must not think that we can keep the good bits while we throw out the bad bits, or that we can embrace a few neutral bits. No, false promises always entice us away from true life. The teaching we consume and the lifestyle we adopt is either drawing us to Christ or it is enslaving us to something else.

Peter's closing denunciation says that false teachers who get us tangled in things other than Christ are actually ensnared themselves. They are worse off than before they falsely professed Christ. Peter's imagery is rather stark and confronting: they are pigs back in the mud, dogs sticking their nose in their own vomit.

But remember, I said I want to show you that when Peter speaks like this it is actually not abrasive but healthy. Here's why: verse 13 calls false teachers "blots and blemishes" feasting within the church. This is serious because the church is Christ's great love, "prepared as a bride adorned for her husband" (Revelation 21:2). His delight in us, and our destiny to be God-echoing people of glory, are the crowning joy and final purpose of our whole existence.

The language of blots and blemishes comes from the Old Testament sacrificial system about offering acceptable worship to God. We are Christ's cherished bride, worshipping him in holiness and bound for a wedding feast when he returns. Blots and blemishes simply will not do. They spoil the bride. We do not want them as we look forward to life with our Lover, and he is passionately committed to removing them from us.

This is why false teaching and waterless springs can never be tolerated, but can only ever be denounced. In fact, to denounce them is the most loving thing to do. To denounce them is to love the church and keep it drinking only from Jesus, the true source of living water. One of the defining marks of a Christian is love. And love defends, protects, and beautifies.

DISCUSSION *10 MINUTES*

What kind of reasoning and evidence is often put ahead of the Bible today, either by you or by people you know? What do you think is happening in the heart when you or others do this?

How comfortable are you with making denouncements of false teaching? What attitudes should you copy from Peter, and what attitudes should you also take care to avoid?

Lesson

ABRASIVE WORDS

20 MINUTES

You might think you aren't likely to fall prey to false teaching. But in fact, it is all around you and it is subtly enticing. Anything your national culture, your family culture, or even your church culture puts its hope in can be a waterless spring. You accept its "teaching." Even though it might not be all bad, you become led by its empty hopes rather than having your hope in Christ.

For this exercise, work on your own to come up with some abrasive but necessary words that denounce those false directions in your life. Complete all three steps below, and then discuss your results with the group.

STEP 1: IDENTIFY FALSE TEACHING. Single out one or two things that might drive your life more than Jesus. You won't necessarily have to tell the group what these are, but you will need to have some specific "waterless springs" in mind as you work through this exercise. Use the prompts below to pick an item or two.

Influences. Instead of being led by the gospel, I often take my cues from things outside the Bible. They may be dressed up to look Christian, but they are actually alternatives to a supernatural hope in Jesus. These might be:

- **Political stances or goals.** A leader, narrative for my nation, or way forward that I can latch onto more readily than to Jesus.
- **Family or friend-group values.** A way my people think or are expected to do things, which can influence me more than Jesus.
- **Popular thinking.** A generally accepted path to happiness, value to affirm, or sign of success in my workplace, school, neighborhood, or the wider culture, which I can buy into.
- **Christian culture.** A widely accepted viewpoint or goal within my Christian community that isn't really derived from the Bible.
- **Entertainment I consume.** A value or way of understanding the world that comes from my daily amusements.
- **Other:** ____.

Desires. Instead of loving Jesus and striving for the joy he gives, I often look for pleasure in the same kinds of things the false teachers in 2 Peter desired. These might be:

- **Money.** The idolizing of security, comfort, opportunity, or standing in the world that is behind greed.
- **Sexual indulgence.** The empty lies about excitement, pleasure, or intimacy that come with lust.
- **Followers.** The hollow promises of approval, image-building, worldly reputation, or just getting noticed.
- **Power.** A desire to have my way or impact the world that consumes me more than Jesus's impact in the world.
- **Other:** ____.

STEP 2: USE SOME ABRASIVE WORDS. Now that you've identified some of your empty desires and non-gospel influences, denounce them. Think of some words or short phrases you can use to expose the stark truth about them. Don't hesitate to use sharp phrasing, like Peter. You need to tell yourself bluntly what these influences and desires really are. Write your abrasive-word list below. You don't necessarily need to fill every line.

____

____

____

____

____

____

STEP 3: USE SOME BEAUTIFUL WORDS. Now that you've denounced your waterless springs, turn your attention to Jesus. He said, "Everyone who drinks of this water will be thirsty again, but whoever drinks of the water that I will give him will never be thirsty again. The water that I will give him will become in him a spring of water welling up to eternal life" (John 4:13–14). So, think of some celebratory words about Jesus and all he gives you. What is praiseworthy about him that stands in beautiful contrast to the influences and desires you denounced? Write your list of words below:

____

____

____

____

____

____

When the group is ready, share some of the words from your two lists. Explain why you chose them. How might those words help you to stay mindful of the difference between false teaching and the gospel of Jesus?

WRAP-UP AND PRAYER *10 MINUTES*

Spend part of your prayer time asking for victory in the fight to resist false influences and evil desires. Remember that this is not a battle you undertake alone, but one you fight in God's power and alongside fellow believers.

Lesson

6

YOUR CREATOR AND JUDGE

BIG IDEA

Jesus will return as the Creator and Judge of the whole world, just as he was the global Creator and Judge at the world's beginning. We should be confident of this and live accordingly.

BIBLE CONVERSATION *20 MINUTES*

Peter has been confronting false teachers who especially denied that Jesus will return to judge the world. In this passage, Peter will mention "the predictions of the holy prophets," who often spoke of that end-times judgment. He will also mention Jesus's commands "through your apostles," who often wrote about how to be godly as we wait for Jesus's return. And he will mention attitudes in "the last days," which usually in the New Testament means the current period between Jesus's ascension to heaven and his return. This means that, once again, this part of 2 Peter is about how we live *now* in light of what we believe will happen *then*.

Have someone read **2 Peter 3:1–7** aloud. Then discuss the questions below:

How well does Peter's goal for his writing, explained in verses 1 and 2, match your goals when you open the Bible to read it? Explain.

Look at Peter's description of scoffers in the last days. How does it compare to the attitude of people you know today?

Outline Peter's argument as he refutes the scoffers. How does his method compare to the way you might respond to people who belittle faith in Jesus?

****

Now take turns by paragraph reading the article aloud. Then discuss the questions that follow.

Lesson

UNEMBARRASSED SUPERNATURALISM

5 MINUTES

Throughout his letter, Peter goes straight to parts of the Bible we might tend to avoid. He brings up accounts we find tricky to explain, or which are even embarrassing, in many cultures today. Creation in six days by the word of God? That's not what science says. A worldwide flood of judgment? It must be an embellished tale about a local event—the fable about the boat won't float. Fire and sulfur on a whole city that was perverting God's design for sex and marriage? That might sound hateful. A talking donkey? Ridiculous.

So we decide, let's not open those cans of worms. Let's not give the skeptics and mockers more fuel. Let's not add to the doubts of doubting Christians. Let's stay on topic. Just stay on Jesus!

But what kind of Jesus do we have if he is not the world's Creator and the worldwide Judge? If Christ is not the God who first created all things with just a word, we can hardly expect he will return to re-create the cursed world we live in now. Or if Christ did not form the first man out of dust, we can hardly expect he will raise our bodies from the dead after they have turned to dust. And if Christ did not flood the whole world in judgment, covering the mountaintops, we can hardly expect he will return to rid us of every shred of evil in the coming life. You see, we keep looking at the beginning because it assures us of the ending. And the ending determines how we live today.

So when Peter is confronted with skepticism about Jesus's return and coming judgment, he goes to creation and the flood. The skeptics wonder where Jesus is if he hasn't shown up yet. Their underlying premise is that God does not, nor cannot, intervene in the world because nothing has changed since the beginning. But their premise deliberately "forgets" how the beginning itself contains the historical facts they claim to be seeking.

First, there's creation. By God's word, he spoke and the waters separated. Then by his word again, he spoke and the waters gathered.* That's how the earth was formed—supernaturally. God created everything from nothing and then began to form and fill his world. He was intimately involved in his creation.

Second, there's the flood. Again God used water, this time to judge the world. And again, the water worked because God had spoken: "For behold, I will bring flood waters upon the earth to destroy all flesh" (Genesis 6:17). The Bible emphasizes the worldwide totality of this, with water high above every mountain.** That's how the earth was destroyed—supernaturally. There are other examples too of God's water-and-word judgment in the Old Testament, like the Egyptians at the Red Sea. But Peter points to the flood because it is a universal event. It is a de-creation of the whole world followed by a re-creation.

For Peter, the creation and the flood are key points in the Bible's plotline. They both indicate there *has* in fact been massive divine intervention in the world. God stepped in once to create the world. He stepped in a second time to destroy the world and re-create it.

* See Genesis 1:6–10.

** See Genesis 7:17–24.

This means he can step in a third time to destroy the world—this time with fire—and create a new heavens and new earth. God will keep his word.

Now let's apply this to skepticism we hear today. Theologian B. B. Warfield is reported to have said, "Christianity is unembarrassed supernaturalism."[4] The adjective is important: *unembarrassed*. How many of us, if we're honest, get a bit embarrassed when some supernatural aspect of the Bible gets brought up at work or school or when we're with friends? Maybe it's the flood, or Jesus walking on water—the kind of things our secular world pokes fun at.

Well, Peter is not embarrassed by any of it. He was present with Jesus when he performed his miracles. He witnessed the transfiguration, walked on water to meet Jesus, and talked with Jesus after his resurrection. The supernatural was real for Peter—he experienced it personally and knew the person behind it. And this is what the church of Jesus Christ needs to recover in our day. We need an unembarrassed confidence in the supernaturalism of Christianity. If we are going to have an impact on the world as we face increasing pressure and questions from our culture, we need to recover our theological nerve. If we are going to hold out to the world, and to our skeptical friends and neighbors, a Savior who really will change everything for them, then we need the Bible's entire supernatural plotline. And isn't this what our skeptical friends and neighbors want? Deep down, they want someone to be honest with them about what the future holds and where their lives are heading. Engaging with them on some of the turning points in the Bible plotline, such as creation and the flood, can help them have a clear perspective on how God is going to act in the future because of how he has acted in the past.

Remember, the beginning assures us of the ending, and how we live is with the end in mind. We will only know as Christians how to live in the present if we are clear and confident about the future.

DISCUSSION *10 MINUTES*

How comfortable are you with the Bible's supernatural parts, especially around unbelievers in your community? Explain.

What end-times truth about Jesus might be encouraging for someone you know to hear? Why would it encourage them?

Lesson

BELIEVING THE COMING MIRACLES

20 MINUTES

As you've seen, from its very start the Bible wants you to be confident that Jesus is both your Creator and your Judge. He is returning to perform these roles in miraculous ways not seen since the beginning times. And your life too is moving toward the day when you will meet Jesus just as he works worldwide creation and judgment again.

Even if you don't openly scoff at this future, it can be hard to live each day as if it really is about to happen, since you don't see it now. For this exercise, read on your own about each end-time truth below. Also read through the descriptions of what your life will look like when you really believe it and when you don't believe it so deeply. Note patterns you see in yourself, and be ready to discuss them.

TRUTH: Jesus the Creator will raise the dead to bodily, never-ending life.

When I really believe this:	*When I don't deeply believe this:*
I lay down my life for Jesus and his kingdom, knowing I will receive much more in return.	I protect my life to the point of selfishness, avoiding dangerous or unpleasant places even though I could be of help.
Even in the face of death, I still have hope and am able to comfort others.	The grief of death destroys my hope or so disturbs me that I try to ignore death.
I approach daily life with the goal of storing up good deeds that will last into the next life, being generous with my money, time, privileges, etc.	I approach life with the goal of getting what I can out of it while I can, seldom being noticeably generous, and angling to be first in line, avoid shortages, etc.
Those I dearly love (like my children) would say my great desire for them is that they find life in Jesus.	Those I dearly love would say I desire some sort of this-world success or happiness for them.

TRUTH: Jesus the Judge will fully deal with everyone who has hurt me, and will do it with perfect justice.

When I really believe this:	*When I don't deeply believe this:*
I am freed to forgive.	I remain enslaved to grudges and anger.
I am freed to be joyful even amid deep hurts.	I remain enslaved to bitterness.
I am freed to be humble, realizing that I too deserve to be judged, which allows me to love mercy.	I resist admitting fault or showing mercy to anyone who can't prove they deserve my kindness.

TRUTH: Jesus the Judge will give eternal punishment to all who align with sin instead of with him.

When I really believe this:	*When I don't deeply believe this:*
I learn to treasure Jesus and to hate sin, treating it as a serious enemy I need to resist daily.	I am casual about sin, seldom truly struggling against it nor sorrowful when I give in to it.
I realize I cannot escape punishment by my own goodness, and I cling in faith to Jesus who took that punishment for me.	I feel little need for Jesus because I don't think I need to escape anything particularly dangerous, just become a somewhat better person.
I become a thankful person who's deeply grateful to Jesus for saving me, is willing to follow him, and dares not despise his love.	I mostly do whatever I want, claiming to follow Jesus but not actually very interested in him or how he says to live.

TRUTH: Jesus the Creator is returning to make an eternal home for me, free of every evil and sadness, where all of God's children will enjoy life with their Father.

When I really believe this:	*When I don't deeply believe this:*
I obey God like a dearly loved child, happy to act like my Father and his family.	I obey God grudgingly, like a hired worker who can't expect love otherwise.
I obey expectantly, eager to start living like the fully righteous person I soon will be.	Growth in holy living holds little excitement for me, feeling more like a burden.
I have a deep interest in Jesus's kingdom and the mission to advance it, knowing what a grand future is ahead for his people and the world.	I have little interest in serving Jesus's kingdom or telling others about him so they can be brought in.

When the group is ready, share some of your thoughts. Where are you living like you believe in Jesus the coming Creator and Judge, and where are you not?

Where would you like to have a firmer *belief* in one of these truths and the changed *behavior* that comes with it?

WRAP-UP AND PRAYER *10 MINUTES*

Prayerfulness is another feature of your life when you deeply believe the truth about Jesus. Prayer is your pipeline to the supernatural, your way of practicing faith and thankfulness, and a satisfying time with your Father in anticipation of your heavenly life. Pray together with these wonders in mind.

Lesson

7

THE DAY OF FIRE

BIG IDEA

We should not get complacent about the return of Jesus, since the coming upheaval will be severe and the opportunity for repentance in the meantime is astounding.

BIBLE CONVERSATION *20 MINUTES*

Peter is answering skeptics who ask about Jesus, "Where is the promise of his coming?" The wait for the second coming has been longer than expected, but Peter has said it will happen just as surely as worldwide creation and judgment happened when the earth was first formed and later flooded. Now he adds more points about the wait and what will happen when Jesus returns on "the day of the Lord," a phrase denoting an event of both God's salvation and his judgment.

Have someone read **2 Peter 3:8–10** aloud, and then discuss the questions below:

Which of Peter's explanations for why Jesus has not yet returned do you find most helpful? Explain why.

Why else can Peter's readers, and you as well, be glad that God is patient?

When Peter says that the works done on earth will one day be exposed, how do you react?

****

Next, read this lesson's article aloud, switching readers with each paragraph. When you finish, discuss the questions that follow.

Lesson

THE END OF THE WORLD

5 MINUTES

No one in history who has predicted the return of Christ or the end of the world has ever gotten it right. You can go online and find lists of such predictions. There have been more than a hundred dating back to the first century. Not one of them has come true, of course.

So, it's no wonder you will find serious skepticism, especially in Western cultures, about predictions concerning the end of the world—including whether it will happen at all. Most people don't even think Jesus rose from the dead. That he's coming again in judgment seems still more farfetched. This is why our passage in 2 Peter is so relevant for us today. It gives us a new perspective on God's coming judgment at the return of Christ. Peter has four points for us to understand.

1. God's timing is not our timing. Yes, Jesus has promised he is coming soon.* But Peter takes us to Psalm 90, where Moses reflects on God's everlasting existence. The psalm says at one point that our lives last seventy or eighty years, but also that compared to God we are like grass that withers in a day. In fact, Moses tells God, "A thousand years in your sight are but as yesterday when it is past" (Psalm 90:4).

* See Revelation 22:7, 12, 20.

What feels like a long time to us is a short time to God. Peter's point is that as we wait for Jesus's return, we need to adopt God's perspective on time. We should live in his time zone, so to speak.

2. God isn't being slow, but patient. In Peter's culture, if a god was slow or delayed, then that god was not in control. It meant something outside of himself hindered him from keeping his promise. But Peter knows God is not running behind time. Rather, it is in God's nature to be patient.

God let Adam live 930 years after eating the forbidden fruit. God waited 400 years, until the sin of the Canaanites was full, before punishing them and taking their land. God waited centuries while Israel's kings committed idolatry before sending his people into exile. God is "slow to anger, and abounding in steadfast love" (Exodus 34:6). He is patient with sinners, and never rushed. A godly Bible teacher whom my mother knew once put it like this: "God moves through history with majestic leisureliness."

Notice how Peter says the Lord is patient "toward you." This means that if you are still alive today, *you* are a beneficiary of God's incredible patience. What are you going to do with it? Will you have contempt for it or repent in light of it? Maybe you've had doubts about the coming judgment. Maybe you've persisted in some pattern of ungodly living you won't repent of. The wait for Jesus to return is not a reason to think you can get away with your sin, or that you can get around to repenting later, but rather a gracious call to repent now.

3. Christ's return will be surprising. We've seen how God is slow to anger and patient in all his judgments. But this does not mean that his patience will never run out. It will. The day Christ returns to enact God's final judgment will be the day God's patience against sinners comes to an end. And when it does, it will be surprising. Peter affirms the certainty of the coming judgment, but this does not mean it will be predictable. Peter recalls Jesus's words about it arriving like a thief in the night.* The point about thieves is that they surprise us. The people throughout history who have thought they could predict Christ's return should have remembered this. And we who are still waiting should understand that the God who moves with majestic leisureliness through history will move with surprising swiftness at the end of history. We need to be ready for it.

4. Christ's return will be exposing. Peter gives us a picture of cosmic upheaval. God will peel back the heavens, like a piece of wrapping paper, exposing the earth and everything done on it. The earth itself won't burn up, but will be like an empty food can tossed into a campfire: the label burns off, exposing the metal beneath. Everything above us will be dissolved as everything around us is laid bare. Every act. Every word. Every thought. God will expose it all, and what he finds he will judge—and justly punish all that is sin.

This alone should be enough to change how we live today, reminding us to make every effort to be godly. It should also change our world-is-ending worries. What great danger does our world face? A coronavirus? Climate change? A strike from a stray asteroid? Planetwide nuclear war? Well, something worse is coming to this earth: the fire of Christ's judgment. Stockpiled food or bomb shelters won't get us through it. We will need a place of far greater safety.

In 2009, massive bushfires erupted in the Australian state of Victoria. More than a hundred people lost their lives, unable to flee the fires fast enough on a day that came to be known as Black Saturday. But one man, unable to find a way out of the fires, instead drove his car onto a burnt piece of ground still smoking from flames that had recently passed through. The only place of safety was where the fire had already been.

On the day Jesus Christ comes to judge this world with fire, the only place of safety will be where the fire of God's judgment has already

* See Matthew 24:42–44.

been. That place is a person, Jesus himself, who "bore our sins in his body on the tree, that we might die to sin and live to righteousness" (1 Peter 2:24). Those of us who are in Christ will not be exposed and then judged; we will be clothed and then welcomed. Jesus is not coming again simply to punish the wicked. He is coming to complete the redemption and restoration that was begun on the cross. The Savior who took the judgment in our place will welcome us into his new heaven and new earth.

DISCUSSION *10 MINUTES*

Do you tend to feel eager for Jesus to return or glad that God is being patient? Why do you think you feel that way?

If you were more attentive to the fact that Jesus is returning and less worried about other threats to the earth, how might you live differently? Explain.

Lesson

EXERCISE

MOTIVES FOR MISSION

20 MINUTES

One way the truth about Jesus's return changes how we live, and how we think about this world, is by motivating us to be part of his mission. The current period of waiting for Christ to come back is also a period of unprecedented gospel-telling. We who know the Godlike life are sent to the whole world with the good news of salvation. We introduce others to Christ, urging them to repent of sin and put their faith in him. And we show how Christ's kingdom has broken through into the present world as we anticipate his arrival to reign fully.

On your own, read through the following descriptions of four motives for mission. For each, ask yourself what aspect of the description feels especially motivating to you. Also consider some way it has led you to be involved in missions in the past, or where it might make you eager to be involved in the future—either a way to go yourself or to help send others. You don't necessarily need a response to every prompt, but do try to come up with a few short answers you can explain to the group.

The URGENCY of the gospel. For everyone who is lost, the fire of God's wrath is coming with surprising swiftness. We want them to get to their only hope from the Person of safety, because there is a stark contrast between the future of those who run to Jesus and those who do not. "They will suffer the punishment of eternal destruction, away from the presence of the Lord and from the glory of his might, when he comes on that day to be glorified in his saints, and to be marveled at among all who have believed" (2 Thessalonians 1:9–10).

One aspect or image of the gospel's urgency that especially makes me want to tell others about Jesus is:

____

____.

One way the gospel's urgency has led me into mission in the past, or one place it could lead me, is:

____

____.

The BEAUTY of the gospel. We love God's offer that all should come to repentance. We treasure the promises of complete forgiveness, adoption as God's children, and a destiny of glorious holiness for all who come in faith to Jesus who lovingly died and lives for us. No message is more beautiful or a greater honor to share. "Then I saw another angel flying directly overhead, with an eternal gospel to proclaim to those who dwell on earth, to every nation and tribe and language and people. And he said with a loud voice, 'Fear God and give him glory, because the hour of his judgment has come, and worship him who made heaven and earth, the sea and the springs of water'" (Revelation 14:6–7).

An aspect of the gospel's beauty that especially makes me want to share it is:

____

____ .

One way the gospel's beauty has led me into mission in the past, or one place it could lead me, is:

____

____ .

The COMPASSION behind the gospel. The Lord in his patient love has waited for us and has found us, and this gives us a similar heart of compassionate service for others. We love the message of mercy for sinners and are eager to share and show it. Jesus said, "I lay down my life for the sheep. And I have other sheep that are not of this fold. I must bring them also, and they will listen to my voice. So there will be one flock, one shepherd" (John 10:15–16).

An aspect of God's compassion that motivates me to mission is:

____

____ .

One way I have moved out in compassion, or one place I might, is:

____

____ .

The coming VICTORY of Christ's kingdom. Jesus has a global purpose: he is coming with a roar to expose sin and to reign in righteousness. We go out into the world knowing that our mission on behalf of Christ is worth any sacrifice and will surely end one day in the complete defeat of evil and in worldwide worship. Jesus said, "Truly, I say to you, in the new world, when the Son of Man will sit on his glorious throne, you who have followed me will also sit on twelve thrones, judging the twelve tribes of Israel. And everyone who has left houses or brothers or sisters or father or mother or children or lands, for my name's sake, will receive a hundredfold and will inherit eternal life" (Matthew 19:28–29).

An aspect of Jesus's coming victory that especially makes me want to be part of his mission today is:

____

____.

One thing I have given up for the sake of Jesus's greater kingdom, or something I might give up, is:

____

____.

When the group is ready, share some of your responses. How does Jesus's pending return motivate you to participate in missions today?

WRAP-UP AND PRAYER *10 MINUTES*

Having just discussed missions, your prayer time might include prayer for missionaries or your own involvement in missions.

Lesson

8

THE WORLD WHERE RIGHTEOUSNESS DWELLS

BIG IDEA

We continually guard the truth, grow in Christ, and seek glory for God, knowing that we are people destined for a world where righteousness dwells.

BIBLE CONVERSATION *20 MINUTES*

Peter has just said that when Christ returns, the heavenly bodies above us will be burned up as the earth and the deeds done on it are exposed for judgment. This is the kind of supernatural event the false teachers scoffed at as they lived by their own sense of right and wrong instead of following Jesus. Earlier, Peter had bolstered his argument by reminding his readers of the Old Testament Scriptures, where prophets predicted the day of the Lord and said it will include world-shaking miracles. Now Peter will add the word of his fellow apostle Paul whose letters he also calls Scripture, and who also wrote about the need to be godly in light of the monumental wonders of the second coming (for instance, see chapters 4 and 5 of 1 Thessalonians). All this will set up Peter's final instructions to his readers.

Have someone read **2 Peter 3:11–18** aloud. Then discuss the questions below:

Look at how Peter describes the people who will dwell in the new heavens and new earth. What do you find appealing about them and how they live?

What does Peter say happens when people twist the Scriptures? When have you seen this occur?

Look at Peter's final instructions in verses 17–18. Why might it be helpful for these to be the last words his readers, including you, hear from him?

****

Now read this study's final article aloud, switching readers at each paragraph. Then discuss the questions at the end of the article.

Lesson

LIVING NOW IN LIGHT OF THEN

5 MINUTES

If we were to put the theme of 2 Peter into a motto, it might be this: living *now* in light of *then*. What we do today is shaped by what we believe about tomorrow. Even humanists and atheists do this. They believe that when they die, they're done, and so they live for progress or pleasure in this life only. Anyone skeptical about Christ's return will serve some other, false god—some desire of their sinful self. Peter wants us to be certain of Christ's return so that we embrace a godly life instead. Live *now* in light of *then*.

A life of "holiness and godliness" (v. 11) is set apart for God and morally upright. It is Godlike, distinctly different. People who know us should be looking at our lives and thinking, "There's something different about you that reminds me of God."

That kind of morally-distinct living is what you do when you know there's a fire coming. If a huge fire were coming toward your house, you wouldn't go on living like people do when there's no fire. Or if you knew a business was about to crash, you wouldn't invest in that business. In the same way, why would we invest in behavior that's heading for God's damnation? It would be total madness.

As we practice holiness instead, Peter says we speed the day of Christ's coming. I don't think this means God changes his plans, since Jesus said the Father knows the day and hour of his return.* But in our minds, the time it seems to take is fluid. A godly life makes the conscience glad. It will mean we no longer dread Christ's return but eagerly begin to anticipate it. Time flies when you're being holy.

And this fast-approaching future is about much more than a coming judgment; it's also about a coming renewal. The earth will survive, having some continuity with the world we inhabit now, but its quality will be entirely new. As Paul wrote in Romans 8:21, "The creation itself will be set free from its bondage to corruption and obtain the freedom of the glory of the children of God." Did you notice how the new creation will be worth waiting for not just because of the place, but also because of the people? Peter agrees when he calls it a world "in which righteousness dwells" (2 Peter 3:13).

That's a beautiful picture of righteousness personified, living in a home. This is not the righteousness of Christ credited to us when we believe, but our own embodied righteousness. It's men and women, boys and girls, who are justified in Jesus and now living fully righteous lives. We will finally be the people we are called to be but fail to be in this world. We will be in our true home. We will be with Jesus who did God's will perfectly, and we will be living like him.

This glorious destiny is why Peter calls us to begin embodying righteousness now. If that's where we are going to live, surely we should start looking like we belong there. Live *now* in light of *then*. It's a bit like if you were going on a summertime trip to the beach. You wouldn't dress like you were headed to work. You would put on sunglasses, something to swim in, and maybe a summery, brightly-colored shirt or floppy hat. Although not at the beach yet, you would look like you belong there. It's the same for all who are headed to the new heavens

* See Matthew 24:36.

and new earth where righteousness dwells. We should live here like we belong there.

So what does this mean for us in an age when people twist the Bible's meaning? The church today is under pressure from false teachers who say we should update our message to fit new sensibilities. This threat has followed the same progression we've seen in 2 Peter:

- It starts with embarrassment about the beginning. Maybe we should treat creation and the judgment-heavy flood as mere myths.
- That leads to embarrassment about the ending. Perhaps we should downplay Jesus the coming, fiery Judge.
- And that leads to embarrassment about what God says is moral behavior. If Jesus is not our Judge, let's modernize our teaching about sex, ungodly lifestyles, or evangelism. Let's bend those touchy parts of the Bible.

We are always just a few steps away from following our own desires instead of our Savior—a few steps from not being dressed for eternity. So Peter calls us to respond to the Bible twisters in two ways. We must be on guard, and we must grow. That's his final word to us: "Take care that you are not carried away with the error of lawless people and lose your own stability. But grow in the grace and knowledge of our Lord and Savior Jesus Christ. To him be the glory both now and to the day of eternity. Amen" (vv. 17–18).

The instruction to grow is interesting. After warning us not to fall for error, we might expect Peter to tell us to stand. He could say, "Hold your ground" or, "Remain firm." But instead, he urges movement. It's like the bicycle illustration from lesson 1. We keep pedaling to stay upright. Peter says to grow in grace, meaning we keep growing in our daily experience of all the saving favor Jesus gives us. And Peter says to grow in knowledge, meaning we keep learning what Jesus tells us about himself through the Bible. This helps us detect false teachers and skeptics.

That's how we fulfill our great glory, which is to reflect Christ's glory. Peter's closing sentence shows us there's something missing from our motto. The theme of 2 Peter should be: live now in light of then *soli Christo gloria*. Live now in light of then *for Christ's glory alone*. That's the Godlike life, and nothing could be better.

DISCUSSION *10 MINUTES*

When people look at you, how can they tell you are headed to a place where righteousness dwells? How would you like to look more heaven-bound to others?

What steps can you take to be on guard and to grow, so you avoid twisting the Bible to fit your own desires?

Lesson

ARE YOU PERSUADED?

20 MINUTES

Throughout his letter, Peter has given you vivid images designed to persuade you. He wants to motivate you to godly living by increasing your confidence in the truth about Jesus. He wants you to be sure about the things to come, the witness of the Scriptures, and the reliability of God.

For this exercise, work on your own to think back on all you've learned from your time in 2 Peter. Each box below mentions one broad topic Peter has addressed. Think of something within that topic that you have learned, come to appreciate better, or become more confident about. Note which of those is the case, and then fill in the box with a few details. You can either write a brief explanation in the box, or you can channel Peter's use of imagery by making a simple sketch. You don't necessarily have to fill in each box, but do have something you can share when the group is ready. If you end up waiting for others to finish, begin thinking through the discussion questions that follow.

Something about the **coming judgment when Jesus returns** that I have . . .

☐ learned

☐ come to appreciate better

☐ become more confident about

Something about the **coming life Christ's people will enjoy** that I have . . .

☐ learned

☐ come to appreciate better

☐ become more confident about

Something about the **Bible and its message** that I have . . .

☐ learned

☐ come to appreciate better

☐ become more confident about

Something about the **character of God** that I have . . .

☐ learned

☐ come to appreciate better

☐ become more confident about

When the group is ready, share and explain some of your responses. How have you become more persuaded about Jesus?

How might your persuasion about Jesus change some aspect of your life today?

When we resist being persuaded to change, it's often because we won't let go of something that serves as a false god to us—perhaps a sinful desire or a controlling fear. How has Peter shown that Jesus is bigger and better than whatever is holding you back?

WRAP-UP AND PRAYER *10 MINUTES*

Pray for each other about the specific ways you want to live *now* in light of *then*. Ask your Father to keep you on guard and growing in the grace and knowledge of your Lord and Savior Jesus Christ.

LEADER'S NOTES

These notes provide some thoughts and background information that relate to the study's discussion questions, especially the Bible conversation sections. The discussion leader should read these notes before the study begins. Sometimes, the leader may want to refer the group to a point found here.

However, it is important that you not treat these notes as a way to look up the "right answer." The most helpful and memorable answers usually will be those the group discovers on its own through reading and thinking about the Bible text. You will lose the value of taking time to look thoughtfully at the text if you are too quick to turn to these notes.

A SPECIAL NOTE ABOUT GOD'S JUDGMENT

Second Peter addresses a number of challenging themes, particularly with regard to God's judgment of false teachers, sin, and evildoers. It is important that we don't soften or skip these themes when we read a book like 2 Peter. At the same time, because 2 Peter speaks to skeptics who are prone to doubt God or dismiss his warnings about the coming judgment, we need to be sure that we understand the importance and rightness of God's judgment on sin. God is holy, righteous, and just, and so he must punish sin. If God did not punish sin, then he would not be true to himself. But God is also gracious and merciful, revealing his love to sinners by sending his only Son to die for them. On the cross, Jesus received the punishment for sin that we deserve. For all those who repent and believe in him, there is no more judgment, wrath, or punishment to come. But for those who refuse to repent and accept God's offer of salvation in Christ, there is only judgment, wrath, and punishment to come. This is why the New Testament writers, including Peter, urge people not to presume upon God's patience but to repent while there is still time: because if they don't repent, they are only storing up for themselves wrath on the day of God's wrath (e.g., Romans 2:5). Peter's letter contains an invitation to repent and receive salvation through Christ, but it also contains a warning to those who don't. The choice is clear: salvation in Christ or judgment without Christ.

There is also another aspect of God's coming judgment. It is part of his plan to renew all things in heaven and on earth. Just as in the past God cleansed the world of wickedness through judgment by flood waters, so in the future, he is going to cleanse the world of wickedness through judgment by fire. God wants to save his people into a new world in which righteousness dwells, and righteousness can't dwell in that new creation if sinners who love wickedness are still present. God is not a petty tyrant, punishing people flippantly because they have made him mad. He is the holy, just, loving, merciful Creator and Redeemer of the world who will stop at nothing—including the sacrifice of his own Son—to create a perfect new world for his people to dwell in.

LESSON 1: MAKING YOUR SALVATION SURE

The opening verses of 2 Peter give one of the Bible's richest descriptions of the life we have in Christ. This life is precious and sure: it is equal to what Jesus gives the apostles, whom he loved so fully (v. 1). It is free: it is granted by Jesus's righteousness, not earned by ours (v. 1). It is inseparable from godliness: we not only know Jesus but share in his own glory and excellence (v. 3). It brings beautiful change: God undoes our corruption and transforms us morally, at an inner-desire level (v. 4). Note that sharing in the divine nature does not mean we become part of the Trinity. The Creator-creature *distinction* between us and God will never be erased, but the Creator-creature *likeness* we were made to share will be perfected. Also note that our destiny is not to escape the physical world itself, but to escape the corruption that is in the world due to sin. The new heaven and new earth will be physically full but empty of evil.

"For this very reason" is an important opening to Peter's list of Christian qualities in verses 5–7. The practice of these qualities, and your group's discussion of them, has a reason: it should flow from an eagerness to embrace the life Christ has already granted. In chapter 2, Peter will describe the false teachers as ignorant, straying, greedy, and sensually indulgent. The qualities here in chapter 1 make a strong contrast.

The reasons Peter gives for being diligent about godliness point to both the here and now and the life to come. Attention to godly living will make us fruitful in this world and also part of the eternal kingdom when Jesus returns. Peter also does not shy away from warnings alongside his positive motivations. He warns that if we fail to practice godliness, we will be ineffective and blind in this life, and will fall rather than enter Christ's kingdom. The gospel presents a stark contrast: a glorious life for all who repent and believe, and destruction for those who don't.

LESSON 2: THE TRUTH ABOUT CHRIST

Peter's impending death makes him relentless about reminding his readers of their life in Christ, perhaps because he wonders if each opportunity to do so will be his last. Death often helps us focus. Whether it's the death of someone close to us or our own soon-to-come death, we see what's most important and urgent. Peter writes with a sense that his letter is not just helpful, but pressing and necessary. It's possible that at this time Peter was also working on his testimony about Christ to Mark, so that his efforts to put the truth about Jesus in front of his readers included his contributions to Mark's Gospel.

The false teaching about Jesus that Peter confronts is remarkably similar to what many people believe or teach today. People readily believe there is a kernel of truth in the testimony God gives us in his Word, but they also believe much of it is cleverly created stories. Peter refutes this by emphasizing the eyewitness nature of the gospel accounts, the fact that God himself has spoken clearly and directly, and the way all of Scripture fits together for a consistent message about Christ. When he calls the prophetic word something "more fully confirmed" (1:19), he probably means that the witness of the apostles and the witness of the Old Testament confirm each other. Neither is better than the other; rather, the certainty of both is intensified when we consider them together.

LESSON 3: DANGEROUS TEACHING

The false teachers Peter confronts are not merely mistaken believers. They are secretive, conspiratorial, and agenda-driven in a way that makes them traitors to Christ. Although they may be sincere in what they believe, they also know they are bringing in outside teaching that will undermine what the apostles taught. And ultimately they are selfish: greedy, exploitative, and wanting to indulge their sensual desires rather than listen to God.

Your group may wonder if these false teachers are actually saved, or if they once were. Peter's insistence on their "destruction" suggests they are not saved, since the word is often used in the New Testament for damnation in hell (for example, Matthew 7:13; Romans 9:22). Still, phrases like "denying the Master who bought them" (2 Peter 2:1) might lead us to think they once were saved but lost their salvation. However, the Bible often speaks of fake believers as if they are insiders. This is because *outwardly* they are a part of the church community and participate in that covenantal life, even though *inwardly* they are not true believers. Think of Judas: the Bible always refers to him as a "disciple" of Jesus because he was in that group. Yet he was not a true disciple and was never really saved but was destined for destruction like the false teachers (see John 17:12; Acts 1:16–20). In the same way, the false teachers never lost their salvation because they never really had it.

LESSON 4: DESTRUCTION AND SHELTER

Although church discipline and examinations of pastors help protect the church from false teaching, Peter wants us to know that the ultimate condemnation for false teachers is in the future. In the end, those who harm others will turn out to have harmed themselves. God's coming judgment is certain, and in case we doubt he is capable of widespread punishment, we should look at the biblical record. Peter's logical argument follows an *if-then* construction. *If* God judged the angels, and *if* he sent the flood, and *if* he destroyed Sodom and Gomorrah, *then* he surely will bring the final judgment also.

However, this judgment features two main elements in verse 9. Yes, the unrighteous receive punishment, but God also knows how to rescue the godly and will do so. In fact, despite picking out some of the Bible's most horrific examples of sweeping punishment, Peter's discussion of those events also emphasizes how God kept righteous men safe. This means God's people have a double comfort when hearing about judgment: the confidence that in Christ we have a sure shelter, and the assurance that all our anxieties and hurts are in his justice-bringing hands.

LESSON 5: ARROGANT MADNESS

Anger that is righteous and good is usually anger *for the sake of others*. Peter's anger arises from his love for God's people who are being led away from Christ and into sin. His passion for the church drives him into deep irony, found throughout this passage: The false teachers mock angels in a way angels would never do. The supposed rationalists are irrational, like animals. Those who claim to be directed by high wisdom are actually enslaved to coarse lust and greed.

The point of the Balaam account is that God both protects his people from harm and reveals the dangerous false prophet to be a fool. Balaam supposedly is spiritually astute, but he can't detect the angel while his donkey can. Lured by money, the "rational" prophet not only ends up arguing with his irrational animal but loses the argument. This connects with what Peter is saying about the false teachers. They've become so driven by greed and lust that they aren't rational any more. It's both damning and deserving of ridicule.

Despite being so irrational, false teaching and our culture's enticements are real and alluring threats to each of us. They appear to offer life, but by offering something other than Christ they draw us away from our Savior and into sin. Proverbs 13:14 says, "The teaching of the wise is a fountain of life." But any hope set on worldly things—even things that may not be bad in themselves—is a waterless spring that cannot give life. Our culture's definitions of happiness, and the "teachers" who spout them, are actually traps that ensnare us. We must cling only to Jesus.

LESSON 6: YOUR CREATOR AND JUDGE

Peter gives us helpful insight into a biblical author's purpose and the value of reading and hearing the Bible. He wants the faith we profess to be a sincere and confident faith by the means of constant reminders of all God has said to us. We do not hear God's Word once and then try to carry on without it. Rather, we repeatedly take it all in, especially the outlandish-but-true promises of the gospel which Peter is defending, so that our minds and lives come to genuinely reflect it.

Scoffers, on the other hand, follow their own desires instead of God's Word. Notice in verse 5 how they deliberately avoid the witness of the Bible. They are not really ignorant of what it says, but they choose not to remember. In Peter's day, the scoffers said worldwide judgment was not coming because nothing in the world had ever happened like that—conveniently forgetting the flood. In our time, a similar thing happens when people claim Jesus could not have risen from the dead because dead people never come alive again. They've deliberately "forgotten" the one piece of historical evidence that contradicts the premise: the evidence that Jesus did come alive after being dead.

Peter is candid about biblical truth when refuting the scoffers. He does not tiptoe around the Bible's most audacious and miracle-affirming claims but makes them the core of his argument. In cultures today where many people are starved of any confidence in things they cannot see, the same approach may be just what they need from us.

LESSON 7: THE DAY OF FIRE

Most of our questions about what it means that Jesus has not yet returned even though he said he is coming soon are answered in this passage of Scripture. We see that (1) God's idea of "soon" is often not the same as ours; (2) God's continued waiting reveals how patient and full of saving love he is as many more people become believers; and (3) the wait means Christ's eventual return will be even more surprising when it finally happens.

Peter's comment that God does not wish for anyone to perish but that all would come to repentance should not be taken to mean that God is frustrated, as if he had a universal salvation wish that's being thwarted. The main thrust of the passage clearly says the opposite: that God is in control of salvation and its timing. Peter simply is explaining the vast extent of God's patience. God is patient toward everyone, even sinners who have followed the false teachers, or the false teachers themselves who have done much damage, or far-flung peoples who have not yet heard the gospel. And he desires to save many of them—all who repent.

The description of Christ's return may require a few explanations. "The heavens" refers to the sky, not the dwelling place of God. Some translations also mention "the elements" being burned up. These are not the elements from the periodic table in chemistry, but rather a technical phrase for the sun, moon, planets, and stars—which is why many translations say, "the heavenly bodies." It's a picture of cosmic upheaval that leaves the earth uncovered while the rest falls away, which is foretold in Isaiah 34:4. "All the host of heaven shall rot away, and the skies roll up like a scroll. All their host shall fall, as leaves fall from the vine, like leaves falling from the fig tree." Scientific theories that say the sun will one day engulf the earth actually have it backward. The sun will dissolve as Christ brings his all-revealing glory to the earth.

LESSON 8: THE WORLD WHERE RIGHTEOUSNESS DWELLS

Peter's depiction of those who believe in the judgment of God is very different from the uptight image often associated with such belief. As people who anticipate a world of perfect righteousness, we are diligent about morality but also at peace, knowing we are beloved of God. Peter has the double blessing of justification and sanctification in view. *At peace* means we have peace with God, knowing Jesus died *for* our sin to make us fully justified before God. At the same time, we are also eager to be found spotless, knowing Jesus also died *to* sin (see Romans 6:10) and is sanctifying us—making us holy. When Jesus saves us, we receive both from him. It's a holistic salvation the Lord is working as he patiently waits to return. Just as you can't stand in the sun and not receive both light and heat, you can't be in the Son and not receive both justification and sanctification from him.

Yet both are often denied by people claiming to be Christian teachers and by churches calling themselves by Christ's name. Today, as in Peter's time, they explain away the supernatural parts of the Bible. They deflect any idea that Jesus died for sin or that it was even really necessary. And not surprisingly, they then decide to follow the culture more than the Bible when it comes to moral behavior. They still use biblical words, but they twist them. They don't mean the same thing Paul and Peter and the other biblical writers meant.

This makes Peter's final words as relevant today as they were when he first wrote them. We must not let ourselves be carried away by twisted, unbiblical teaching. Instead, we must stay near to Jesus and grow in the miracle-affirming, sin-canceling, soul-winning, and evil-overcoming message of the gospel.

NOTES

1. C. S. Lewis, *The Weight of Glory and Other Addresses* (New York: HarperOne, 2001), 45.

2. John Calvin, *Commentaries on the Catholic Epistles*, trans. John Owen (Grand Rapids: Christian Classics Ethereal Library), vii.ii.i, https://ccel.org/ccel/calvin/calcom45/calcom45.vii.ii.i.html.

3. Peter H. Davids discusses the likely Epicurean influence on the false teachers in *The Letters of 2 Peter and Jude* (Grand Rapids: Eerdmans, 2006), 133–36.

4. Cited in Ian Hamilton, *Ephesians, The Lectio Continua: Expository Commentary on the New Testament* (Grand Rapids: Reformation Heritage, 2017), 258–59.

SELECTED BIBLIOGRAPHY

The content of this book is based on a sermon series I preached as a minister at Cambridge Presbyterian Church and at other churches and conferences since. My sermon preparation was informed by the following commentators, and their influence at different points is reflected in this book.

Bauckham, Richard. *2 Peter/Jude*. Word Biblical Commentaries. Fort Worth, TX: Word, 2000.

Calvin, John. *Hebrews and 1 & 2 Peter*. Translated by William B. Johnston. Calvin's New Testament Commentaries. Grand Rapids, MI: Eerdmans, 1994.

Davids, Peter H. *The Letters of 2 Peter and Jude*. The Pillar New Testament Commentary. Grand Rapids: MI: Eerdmans, 2006.

Gardner, Paul. *1 & 2 Peter & Jude: Christians Living in an Age of Suffering*. Rosshire, Scotland: Christian Focus, 2013.

Lucas, Dick and Christopher Green. *The Message of 2 Peter & Jude*. The Bible Speaks Today. Nottingham: InterVarsity, 1995.

My thanks to Jack Klumpenhower for his excellent editorial assistance in preparing this manuscript.